D1480340

Living on a
Caribbean Island

Louise and Richard Spilsbury

Chicago, Illinois

© 2008 Raintree
Published by Raintree,
a division of Reed Elsevier Inc.
Chicago, Illinois

Customer Service   888–454–2279

Visit our website at www.heinemannraintree.com

Designed by Richard Parker and Manhattan Design
Printed and bound in China by SCPC

12 11 10 09 08
10 9 8 7 6 5 4 3 2 1

Library of Congress Cataloging-in-Publication Data
Spilsbury, Louise and Richard.
Living on a Caribbean island
p. cm. -- (World cultures)
Includes bibliographical references and index.
ISBN-13: 978-1-4109-2819-1 (library binding–hardcover)
ISBN-10: 1-4109-2819-5 (library binding–hardcover)
ISBN-13: 978-1-4109-2828-3 (pbk.)
ISBN-10: 1-4109-2828-4 (pbk.)
1. Caribbean Area--Social life and customs--Juvenile literature. 2. Creoles--Caribbean Area--Social life and customs--Juvenile literature. I. Spilsbury, Richard. II. Title.
F2169.S75 2007
972.9--dc22
                    2006037143

Acknowledgments
The publishers would like to thank the following for permission to reproduce photographs: Alamy Images pp. 23 (Donald Nausbaum), 5 (Oliver Benn), 8 (Sylvia Cordaiy Photo Library Ltd); Art Directors & Trip/ Paul Joynson-Hicks p. 25; Corbis pp. 22 (Blaine Harrington III), 12 (Bob Krist), 15 (Christian Liewig/ Liewig Media Sports), 10 (David Cumming; Eye Ubiquitous), 21 (Peter Turnley), 7 (Philippe Giraud); Harcourt Education Ltd/ Devon Olugbena Shaw p. 14; Getty Images/ Stone/ Matt Henry Gunther p. 4; Harcourt Education Ltd/ Tudor Photography pp. 26, 27 (top and bottom); Nature Picture Library/ Jane Burton p. 11; Panos Pictures pp. 13 (Duncan Simpson), 19 (Rob Huibers); Photographers Direct/ Wandering Spirit Travel Images p. 24; Photolibrary/ Animals Animals/ Earth Scenes p. 20; Photolibrary/ Bill Bachmann Photography p. 18; Robert Harding Picture Library pp. 9 (James Gritz), 28 (Reinhard Dirscherl), 17 (Sergio Pitamitz); Still Pictures/ Achim Pohl p. 16; World Pictures p. 29.

Cover photograph of young woman in costume, celebrating carnival, reproduced with permission of Corbis/ Blaine Harrington III.

Illustrations by International Mapping.

Carnival headdress on pp. 26–27 devised and made by Natalie Abadzis.

Every effort has been made to contact copyright holders of any material reproduced in this book. Any omissions will be rectified in subsequent printings if notice is given to the publishers.

The publishers would like to thank Gwyneth Harold for her assistance with the preparation of this book.

Contents

Some words are printed in bold, **like this**. You can find out
what they mean on page 31.

Caribbean Islands

There are many beautiful islands spread across the clear Caribbean Sea. Islands are areas of land surrounded by water. In the Caribbean one group of islands forms the country of Guadeloupe (see map on page 6).

◄ This Caribbean family lives in Guadeloupe. Like most people in Guadeloupe, they are Creole people.

CARIBS

Caribs are the tribe (group) of people who first settled in the Caribbean. The Caribbean Sea is named after them.

Island history

Many different people have lived on Guadeloupe. The first people came from South America 1,000 years ago. People from France arrived about 500 years ago. France still rules Guadeloupe. The French brought **slaves** from Africa to work for them. Slaves are people with no freedom. Later, Chinese and Indian people also came here.

Creoles are related to the different people who lived on Guadeloupe in the past. Some Creole families have left the islands and moved to other countries, such as the United States.

◄ Many Creole families in Guadeloupe grow bananas. They are sold to people in other countries.

Tropical World

Guadeloupe and the other Caribbean islands are **tropical**. Tropical places always have hot weather.

Island life

Plants grow well in tropical places. The tall trees are filled with birds and insects. Coconut palm trees grow on sandy beaches. Colorful fish swim around **coral reefs**. Coral reefs are rock-like structures in the sea. They are built by small animals called corals.

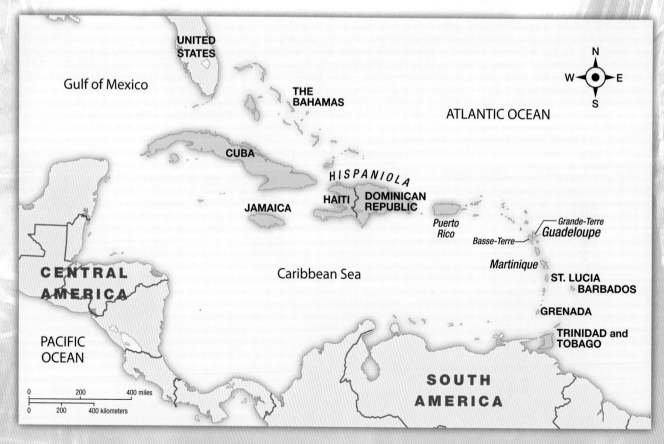

▲ The Caribbean islands make a curved line. The Caribbean Sea lies between this curve and the coasts of Central and South America.

Guadeloupe islands

Guadeloupe is made up of nine islands. The biggest are Basse-Terre and Grande-Terre. Basse-Terre is a hilly island. It was formed from rock that came out of underwater **volcanoes**! Grande-Terre is a flat island. It was made from enormous, ancient coral reefs.

▶ Hurricanes can blow down houses and trees. They sometimes hurt people.

Hurricane season

There are two seasons in the Caribbean. It is dry from February to June. From July to January it rains. **Hurricanes** often happen in September. These powerful storms blow across the Caribbean islands. People on Guadeloupe and other Caribbean islands prepare for hurricanes. They get their boats out of the water and take shelter away from the coast.

At Home

Many **Creoles** on Guadeloupe live in villages. Their homes are square **bungalows**. The windows have shutters with slats. These keep the rooms cool. Many bungalows are made of concrete. This stops them from blowing down in **hurricanes**.

Inside and out

Creole homes are simple. Most have a stove, a TV, a radio, and a refrigerator. Outside there is a yard where people grow fruits, herbs, and other plants. Some people keep hens to lay eggs.

◄ Many Guadeloupe houses are painted in bright, cheerful colors.

Around the village

Many villages were built around old **plantations**. Plantations are farms where plants, such as bananas and sugar, grow. Each village has a church and a school. There is often a grand stone house, where a rich landowner would have lived.

Today, many visitors come to the islands. New hotels have been built for them to stay in.

▼ Big towns by the coast have old forts. They were used to defend islands against unwelcome pirates!

Dinnertime!

Creole food is a delicious mixture of tastes. These come from all over the world!

Traditional foods

Most foods are grown on the islands. People cook and mash local vegetables, such as **cassava** and **yam**. They flavor food with spices from the forest. They drink juices from guava and pineapple fruits.

Creole people also eat seafood. They barbecue fish, such as red snapper, on an open fire. They also cook fish in milk taken from coconuts. They eat the meat of giant **conches**, shellfish, and octopus.

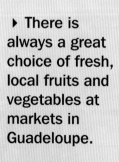

▶ There is always a great choice of fresh, local fruits and vegetables at markets in Guadeloupe.

▲ People catch land crabs to eat. They hunt at night by shining flashlights at the crabs. This blinds a crab for a moment so that people can pick it up.

International meals

The people who settled in Guadeloupe brought foods from their countries. French people brought croissant pastries. Indians brought spices. Today, a curry called chicken colombo is one of the national dishes.

Now, you can even buy burgers and pizza from fast food cafés.

Each **Creole** family is different. Sometimes children, parents, and grandparents live together. Other children live just with their mother. In every family, the people always help each other out.

Work

Many people work on their own farms or on bigger **plantations**. They grow fruit, coffee, cocoa, or spices. Others work in factories where fruits are packaged in bottles or cans. Some people work on mines in the hills or on fish farms near the coast.

People also find work in hotels and restaurants. They make souvenirs for tourists or take tourists on boat trips. Some tourists dive and snorkel around the **coral reefs**.

▲ Many tourists come to the Caribbean. They enjoy the warm, sunny weather, the beautiful beaches, and the tasty food.

▶ Lots of Caribbean people go to church. They get dressed up every Sunday.

WORSHIP

African **slaves** were brought to the Caribbean. Europeans made them pray at **Christian** churches. Their **descendants** were also taught to be Christians. Descendants are a person's children, grandchildren, and younger relatives.

Getting Together

Whenever people meet in Guadeloupe, they shake hands. They also kiss each other on the cheeks.

Women often talk to each other at the market. They go there to sell the food they grow. Men may play dominoes together. Many people also meet at the beach. On Sunday, families gather in church.

▲ The town square is a favorite meeting place. It is often bustling with people. These boys are playing dominoes.

◄ People talking on island radio stations speak in *patois*.

Creole languages

The main language in many Caribbean islands is French. In schools, classes are taught in French. Signs across the islands are also in French. But most **Creole** people talk to each other in *patois*. *Patois* is a mix of European and African languages.

Patois changes from island to island. The *patois* spoken on Guadeloupe sounds different from the *patois* on the island of Jamaica.

ISLAND RADIO

The different islands can be far apart. People listen to radio stations to find out what is happening. They hear island news shows and interviews with local people. Other stations play music by Creole musicians.

Dressing Up

Creole people wear clothes that help them stay cool. They wear T-shirts and shorts or skirts. They often wear flip-flops on their feet.

▶ Most Creole children wear uniforms for school, but they wear what they like in the evenings and on the weekend.

FLAG IT UP!

Many Caribbean people proudly wear clothes in the colors of their flag. The Jamaican flag is black, gold, and green. Grenada's flag is red, green, and gold.

Traditional costume

Slaves used to wear fancy outfits to celebrate major holidays. Women wore bright, colorful skirts with white shirts. They also wore headscarves folded into special shapes. These **traditional** clothes are still worn at festivals and celebrations today.

After slavery was banned, Indian people came to the islands. They brought checked cotton. This material is also popular in island costumes.

▲ Creole women tie their colorful headscarves in many different ways.

At School

On Guadeloupe, all children must go to school from the age of six to seventeen. Most schools start and finish early. This means that children can learn before the hottest time of the day.

▸ Even the school uniforms are colorful in Guadeloupe!

School subjects

Children learn the usual school subjects, such as history, math, science, and languages. Many also have lessons in dance and drama. They learn **traditional** dances such as the *quadrille*. *Quadrille* was originally a French dance. Children also learn dances that are used at carnivals.

◀ Creole children rehearse a song and dance that they will perform at the end of the semester.

SPEAKING

Creole children learn French at school. This can make it easier for them to get jobs in the future. Some teachers speak **patois** to make sure children can understand them.

Time Out!

Caribbean people do lots of fun outdoor activities. They have barbecues on beaches and play games such as volleyball. Around Easter most islanders in Guadeloupe watch the annual soccer match against Martinique. Martinique is a neighboring island (see map on page 6).

▲ There are many things to do by the Caribbean Sea. People can swim, snorkel, surf, or go boating.

▶ Modern Caribbean music is a mixture of sounds and rhythms from France, England, Spain, and Africa.

PARTY!

Zouk is the Creole word for "party." It is also a popular type of dance music in Guadeloupe. It is a mixture of *gwo ka* rhythms and rock guitar.

Music

Music fills the air in the Caribbean. One of the oldest music styles is *gwo ka*. *Gwo ka* means "big drums." The drums are played in different rhythms to accompany songs.

Dancing

The limbo dance is often done for fun on the beach. People lean back and try to dance under a horizontal pole. The limbo stick reminds **Creole** people of the time when African **slaves** traveled to the Caribbean. The slaves came on ships and had to go down into very low holds (decks).

21

Carnival!

Nearly every Caribbean island has big carnivals. They last for days! People join in with costumed parades, dancing, feasting (eating), and fun!

◄ These children are taking part in a children's carnival.

Mardi Gras

The biggest carnival on Guadeloupe is *Mardi Gras*. This is during the dry season, before the rains and storms come. The carnival happens in the period before Easter. This is an important time for **Christian** people.

Sights and sounds

Mardi Gras starts on a Sunday with a parade. For four days there are parties, dances, music, singing, and a costume competition.

The music includes **steel bands**. Steel bands are groups who play metal oil drums. The music first came from the Caribbean island of Trinidad.

The festival ends on Wednesday with the burning of *Vaval*, a giant puppet. *Vaval* is the symbol of carnival.

▶ People dress up as devils in this Easter carnival.

MIXING CULTURES

Mardi Gras brings together different **cultures**. It uses dances, costumes, and traditions from Africa. It also follows the Easter timetable. European settlers brought Easter to the islands.

Remembering the Past

All Saints' Day is a **Christian** festival on November 1. It is when **Creole** people remember their dead loved ones.

Sharing memories

On All Saints' Day, families eat special foods, such as land crab with rice. Families gather to share memories about their **ancestors**.

▲ Before All Saints' Day, people visit cemeteries. They clean up family burial plots. On the day, they light candles on gravestones.

Stories

In the past, storytellers traveled between villages in West Africa. They shared tales and music. Today, older people in the Caribbean tell stories in *patois* on All Saints' Day. They also play *gwo ka* drums.

▲ Some stories are about African animals, such as monkeys and lions. Others describe events from Creole history, such as slavery.

ANANCY

Anancy (or Anansi) is a character in Caribbean stories. He first appeared in West African **slave** tales. He is sometimes a person. More often, he is a clever spider! In some stories, Anancy tricks wild animals. Other stories are about him saving slaves from danger on **plantations**.

25

Make a Carnival Headdress!

The headgear worn at carnivals is colorful and interesting. You can wear it or you can use it to decorate a room!

People wear many types of headgear at Caribbean carnivals. The various types all follow African traditions. They use natural objects, such as grasses, wooden beads, feathers, and shells. Feathers are often used in African masks. People believe feathers help get rid of their problems and pains.

To make a carnival headdress, you will need:

- construction paper
- feathers
- small pom-poms
- sequins
- glitter
- glue
- stapler
- scissors
- pencil.

Step 1

Draw a design on the paper lightly in pencil. Extend the parts that will go around your head. Then, cut it out. Make sure the headband fits your head and there is enough paper to staple together after you have decorated it (see picture).

Step 2

Now, the fun starts! Decorate your headdress with feathers, pom-poms, glitter, and sequins. Ask an adult to staple the two ends together to fit the headdress around your head.

Did You Know?

- Every year millions of people eat Caribbean seafood, spices, and crops, ranging from bananas to coffee.

- The Caribbean Sea and the islands are home to many different species (kinds) of animals. There are turtles, crocodiles, parrots, hummingbirds, whales, dolphins, and more. There are also some of the finest **coral reefs** in the world.

- Millions of visitors from all over the world come to experience the **Creole culture**, nature, and the warm weather.

- Caribbean music is listened to around the world.

▶ Many tourists visit the Caribbean to go diving and see the colorful world beneath the waves.

Island names

Christopher Columbus (1451–1506), an Italian explorer, named Guadeloupe after a **Christian** saint. Its Carib tribe name was *Karukera*. *Karukera* means "island of beautiful waters."

Other ancient names for Caribbean islands describe what they are like. For example, *Xaymaca* (pronounced "Jamaica") means "land of wood and water." This is because of the forests and rivers in Jamaica.

Lere was the early name for Trinidad. It means "land of the hummingbird." This is because lots of hummingbirds live there.

▶ The Caribbean islands are home to nearly 30 million people. The people have different backgrounds and a mix of cultures.

Find Out for Yourself

Books to read

Bojang, Ali Brownlie. *Letters from Around the World: Jamaica*. North Mankato, Minn.: Cherrytree, 2004.

Hallworth, Grace. *Sing Me a Story! Song and Dance Stories from the Caribbean*. Atlanta: August House, 2002.

McDermott, Gerald. *Anansi the Spider*. Norwalk, Conn.: Weston Woods, 2006.

Websites

To read some Anancy stories, look at these websites:

www.historyforkids.org/learn/africa/literature/anansi.htm

www.manteno.k12.il.us/WebQuest/elementary/LanguageArts/Anasi/anansiresourcepage.html

Glossary

ancestor relative, such as a great-grandparent, from a long time before

bungalow home that is built on only one level

cassava potato-like root of a plant, used in cooking and making cakes

Christian person who follows the Christian religion and believes in Jesus Christ

conch sea creature with a spiral shell

coral reef rock-like structures built by small animals called corals

Creole Caribbean person whose ancestors were European, African, or Indian

culture way of life of a society

descendant child, grandchild, great-grandchild, and so on, of a particular family

hurricane powerful, spinning wind that can cause terrible damage

patois local Caribbean language

plantation large area of land in a tropical place where crops (such as bananas or coffee) are grown

slave person who is forced to work for someone else against his or her will. Slaves are given little or no money.

steel band Caribbean music band that plays steel drums made from oil drums

traditional story or way of doing something that has been the same for many years

tropical hot area of the world near the equator (an imaginary line around the middle of Earth)

volcano opening in Earth's surface where melted rock pours out. It often hardens to form a cone-shaped mountain or island.

yam vegetable that grows underground in hot countries

Index